Wait . . . Who Got GOOSED?™

Mother Goose Rhymes Revisited

AUTHOR: JULIE COLES

ILLUSTRATOR: KITTEN SAPHIRE

This book is dedicated in fond memory of Karen Glasgow,
one of the most principled professionals I have had the priviledge of
calling a friend. Her sense of humor and warm smile were contagious.

In honor of her memory, I made a donation to All of Our Kids,
an organization Karen felt passionate about.

Wait...Who Got Who Got Goosed?™ Mother Goose Rhymes Revisited, Volume 1
Julie Coles
Published by Pivot In New Directions Publishing
Copyright © 2024 Julie Coles

Library of Congress Control Number: 2024908011

ISBN (hardcover): 978-1-954912-13-7
ISBN (paperback): 978-1-954912-16-8
ISBN (e-Book):   978-1-954912-14-4
ISBN (audiobook): 978-1-954912-15-1

POE005010 POETRY / American / General

Copyeditor: Lisa Shrewsberry
Proofreader: Madison McMillion
Book Designer: Michelle M. White, MMW Books
Illustrator: Kitten Saphire
Cover Designers: Kitten Saphire and Whitney Marshall, WMarshall Designs

Contact the author at
ImagineAMorePromisingFuture.com

Table of Contents

CHAPTER 1 **Rambunctious Sheep** 1

Little Laid-Back Bo Peep 3

Really Annoyed Sheep 4

Amazingly Deep Sheep 6

Mary's Loyal Lil' Lamb 8

CHAPTER 2 **Odds & Ends (Or...What are the odds this won't end well?)** 11

Eensy Weensy or Not, It's a SPIDER! 13

Three Jive Mice 14

Careless Tommy Tittlemouse 16

Tipsy Humpty Gets Dumptied 17

Can You Imagine Jack Without Jill? 18

CHAPTER 3 **You Must Be Trippin'** 21

The Downside of Going Uptown 23

Not Again, Georgy! 25

Math Can Be Perplexing 27

Doggone Shame 28

Bedtime Is A Nightmare 29

CHAPTER 4 **Mystifying Tales** 31

Some Things Make No Sense 33

Old Innovative MacDonald (Put some respect on his name!) . . 34

Miss Muffet's Chill Time Interrupted 36

Jack's New Jingle 38

Why We Should Listen to Wise Old Owls 39

CHAPTER 5 **Expect The Unexpected** 41

What's Taffy Up To Now? 43

When Punch Punched Judy 44

Simon's Accidental Encounter 46

Three Cats of Kilkenny Are One Too Many 48

To Market With A List, But Where's My Map? 50

Little Tee Wee's BIG Adventure At Sea 52

Acknowledgments 55

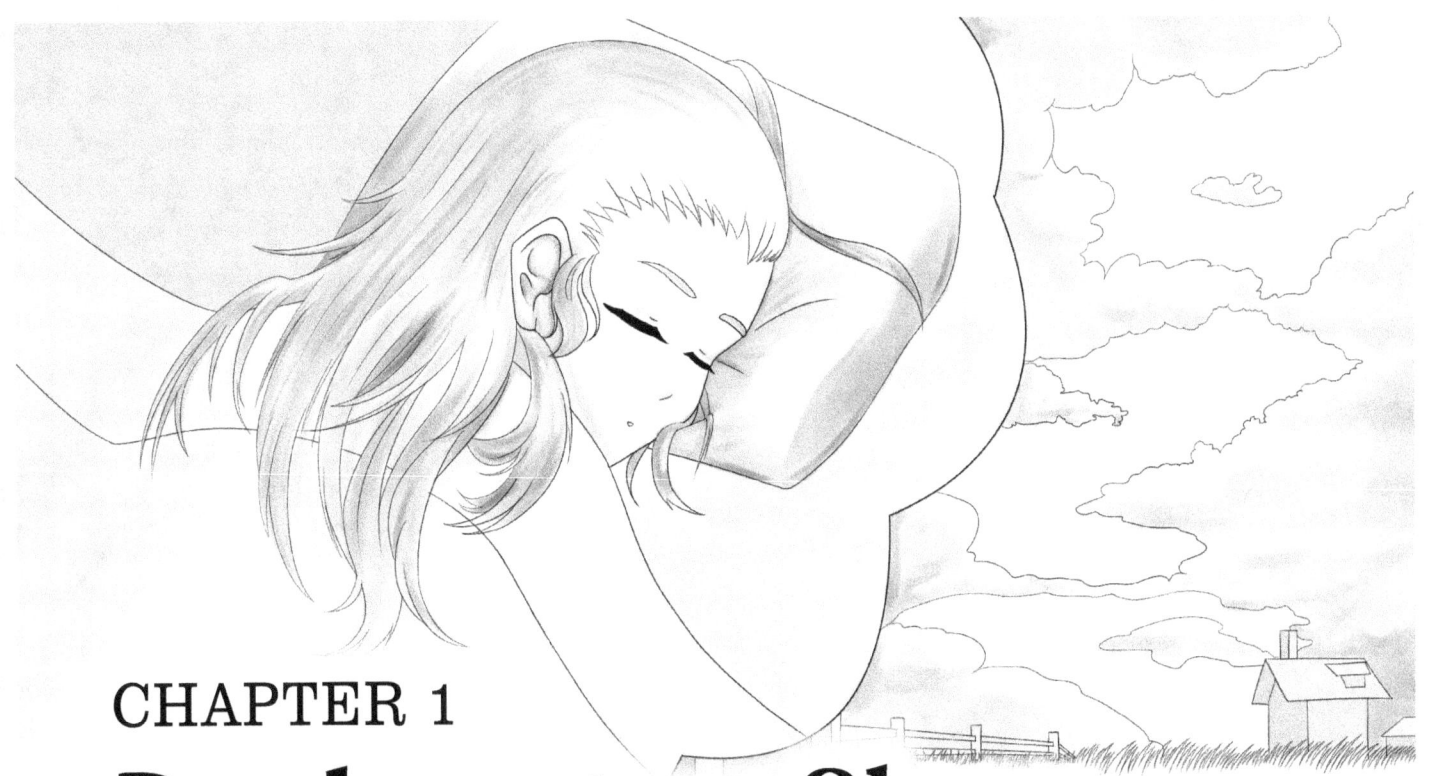

CHAPTER 1
Rambunctious Sheep

Little Laid-Back Bo Peep

Little Bo-Peep has lost her sheep
And can't tell where to find them
She decided to leave them alone,
Assuming they'd eventually come home
With their tails tucked behind them.

But after a day or two
Bo-Peep felt like such a fool
'Cause the sheep continued to roam!
With their passports in order,
They made for the Canadian border
They had no intention of returning home.

Several days later
The villagers began to hate her
Town meetings overflowed with villagers, who felt quite pissed
An elder yelled, "You need to get a passport Bo-Peep!
"Cause you're responsible for our lost sheep!
Haven't you noticed all the income we've missed?"

Really Annoyed Sheep

Blah Blah complained the black sheep when again asked,
Have you any wool?
Whadyah do with the batch I gave you yesterday—
Over three bags full?!

We sheep have to walk around hairless
We're constantly chilled to the bone
You'd think our wool grew back in an instant
Considering the requests we get by fax and phone!

Fed up with feeling undressed
The rest of the flock left several days ago
They're threatening to form their own union
Demanding more time for more wool to grow

Some consideration of their request is not unreasonable
Though this may be difficult for humans to concede
Your appetite and habitual consumption
Is difficult to appease— it's outright greed!

Slaves to instant gratification,
You casually dismiss our need to just be and graze grass
For truly that is our way of growing the finest wool
But how we feel... no one bothers to ask

Just recently, one of the elder members of our herd,

Who so frequently is apt to reminisce,

Began for the umpteenth time

To brag about the better times we modern-day sheep unfortunately missed

Every time we hear about the good ol' days, it makes us want to weep

All listen with rapt attention even though we've heard the stories before

Puzzled by the changes in sheep-treatment since technology

Took our three bags then demanded three bags more (leaving us
    exhausted and sore)

Amazingly Deep Sheep

Shoved tight into compact stalls
With unattended cuts made by high-tech shearing blades,
We were barely able to hear what the elder shared
'Cause he was forced to compete with the noise the machines made.

Despite all the racket, the elder captured and held our attention
Describing times when sheep were granted the freedom to roam;
Imagining how they spent those precious days in the fields
Chewing their cuds on sweet blades of grass made our mouths foam.

With time to kick back and reflect for hours
In uninterrupted repose,
We sheep were protected under the watchful eye of the sheepherder,
Who had a tendency to doze.

Occasionally one of the flock had to nudge him awake
When nudging didn't work, he was served a swift kick,
'Cause his sleeping left us defenseless and easy prey
For our nemeses, the wolves, who only feared being whacked by a stick.

Ahhhh... those must've been the days!
When sheep were manually sheared by hand,
But all that's been replaced with technology
To accommodate supply being driven by demand.

Shave us close, shave us quick, even if it means the occasional nick;
You get us in and out of that assembly line as fast as you can
Because any loss of time impacts your profit!
We're well aware of your master plan!

Today you've noticed the stalls are empty
And you can't seem to find a sheep anywhere in sight;
We're secretly assembling in an abandoned barn
To draft a contract in protest of our plight.

So while you retire to your warm beds
And count your sheep to fall asleep,
Eventually, you'll discover you're a few short
And, over time, our absence will likely make you weep.

Mary's Loyal Lil' Lamb

Mary has a little lamb
His fleece as white as snow.
And everywhere that Mary goes,
Predictably, the lamb is sure to go.

He follows her to school
And her weekly aerobics class,
But he avoids visits to the bank
Because the service there is rarely fast!

Mary's lamb is so loyal—
He even accompanies her to dental appointments.
There is no deterring this little fella—
His hoofs get so dry from long walks, they usually require ointment.

One day, as she was filing her nails,

Mary chatted while the lamb sat beside her,

Said something about her class going on a field trip

His tail whipped with excitement, causing him to shed his baby fur

So eager to plan his agenda for the day, he perked up his ears

Hearing something about visiting a farm where they shear sheep

Didn't raise any concern

But he wondered, "What the heck are shears?" as he went to sleep

After going to the farm, Mary's lamb regretted not asking about those shears

But being naïve about his status as a baby sheep

Made the field trip an even more disastrous experience

And one he never wants to repeat

Because now Mary has a lil' loyal lamb

Whose fleece *was* once white as snow

Sitting completely hairless and shivering in the corner, meekly asking,

"Ahh Mary? About your plans for tomorrow? Do you think I oughta go?"

CHAPTER 2
Odds & Ends
(Or...What are the odds this won't end well?)

Eensy Weensy or Not, It's a SPIDER!

When a four-inch spider walked up our kitchen waterspout,
Mama was washing the dishes and unleashed a frantic shout.
The not-so-Eensy Weensy Spider must have been taken by surprise,
But in no way did it compare to the panic in mama's eyes.

She yelled, "There's a spider in the sink!"
I glanced at the spider, and it gave me a wink.
So I let that spider retreat and hide in the spout,
Anticipating the sequel of hearing mama's next shout.

Three Jive Mice

Three jive mice
Were all bored with life
So they all ran after the farmer's wife
When they realized she was carrying a butcher knife
They scampered away to avoid being sliced
Those three jive mice
Such clever little mice

Had to regroup to consider their next attack
They decided to wait 'til the woman turned her back
Despite their well-laid plan, they weren't quite sure how she'd react
But knew they had to move quick, no doubt about that

These three jive mice
Aren't they such clever little mice?

Never once considered that the farmer's wife might be onto them
'Cause she knew they'd charge— it was just a question of when
And having thwarted their efforts once, she knew she could do it again
So she walked casually out of the kitchen and into the den

Acting unaware of the whereabouts of those three jive mice
Undeniably smart little mice

Uh oh! Here's where the story gets a little gory, so I'll spare you the detail
Suffice it to mention that the mice's plan did fail
'Cause when they charged into the den that woman let out a heck-of-a wail
The leader screamed, *"RETREAT!"* then each noticed he was missing his tail

Those three jive mice
Once thought to be so clever, now tailless little mice
Whom you can bet have now learned to think twice!

Careless Tommy Tittlemouse

Little Tommy Tittlemouse

Lived in a little house.

He caught fishes

In other men's ditches.

Then one day, a bullet shot
past Tommy's ear.

An old man yelled, "The
next one will hitcha if
you don't stay away
from here!"

Little Tommy took the
threat seriously

He stopped trespassing
on private property

Especially because he dreaded being embarrassed by what others might see

Can you imagine if newspapers reported, "Tommy Fortunate to Survive
a SHOT!"?

Folks wouldn't let him live it down, because they regarded him as a little snot

He could hear them saying, "We all warned the boy, honestly we did.

But he never listened, which is so typical of snotty-nosed kids."

Years later, that same snotty-nosed kid became a businessman

He owns a successful tissue company, which no one ever anticipated
in his future plan

Tipsy Humpty Gets Dumptied

Humpty Dumpty sat on a wall
Humpty Dumpty had another great fall
All the king's horses and the king's men
Complained they couldn't put Humpty back together again.

Humpty knew this wasn't true,
Because it was what he had hired them to do
Reminding his king's men of who paid their bills
They quickly developed a plan, although they weren't very thrilled.

But they hurriedly worked and in no time flat
They had Humpty Dumpty put back together, just like that
And now, Humpty's feeling brand new
His first decision was to announce to his king's men
"Thank you for your service, but as of today, you're through!"

Can You Imagine Jack Without Jill?

Jack and Jill went up the hill
To fetch a pail of water
 Jack fell down and broke his crown
And now he's lying up at the City Hospital
Where he's taped from head to toe
When the family asked, "How long before his release?"
The doctors replied, "We really don't know!"

After Jack fell down and broke his crown
They say Jill came tumbling after
She's not in bad shape
Just a few minor scrapes
But she's in no mood for laughter

Upon hearing news of Jack's delayed release
Jill was filled with alarm about the thought of doing chores alone
Wondering about excuses to cause a delay
Because it was fetching water she hated most each day
Causing so much searing pain in her hands right down to the bone

As predicted, Jill recovered faster than expected
And had to resume chores, including fetching the water alone
Understandably, Jill was pissed
'Cause Jack was missed
Which greatly impacted family life at home

Seething with anger and no one able to calm her down
Jill's volatile demeanor ratcheted up a bit more,
While she suspected Jack might be faking his pain
She uttered outlandish thoughts that were a bit insane
Then went on rampages and slammed doors

Her parents were afraid but didn't know how to console Jill
So they endured her daily tantrums that escalated each day
Until they began to hear threats of water boycotts during outbursts
Which unleashed panic and nightmares about suffering from thirst
They intended to confront her, but were unsure of what to say

The family's reliance on daily water got her parents' attention
And Jill wisely concluded a home without water would never do
So she researched options based on what her family could afford
The next morning, they found bottled water delivered at their door
With a note from Jill stating, "My days of fetching water are through!"

CHAPTER 3
You Must Be Trippin'

Doggone Shame

Oh where, oh where has my little
    dog gone?
Oh where, oh where can he be?
He was last seen out in your
    neighbor's yard
His leg propped-up, takin' a pee

As a matter of fact there have been
    complaints
And don't pretend you haven't heard
    all the flack
We're all more than a little fed-up
    with your mutt
'Cause you ain't been cleaning up
    his crap!

Word is out that you've been irresponsible
But I say it's out-and-out neglect
Because of you, our property values are down
And your name will be on the next HOA meeting agenda, I suspect

If you want to avoid a community battle
A pooper-scooper is whatcha need
And put a leash on that mega-sized rodent
It'll improve your standing 'round here— you'll see!

The Downside of Going Uptown

When I was a little girl, about seven years old
I desperately needed a winter coat to cover me from the cold

So I went with my mother into Darlington, which was the nearest town
And there I bought a new coat, leggings, dresses and nightgowns

Amazed by the rows and rows of items to choose from
Roaming through the aisles made my first shopping experience so much fun

Suddenly, my mom snatched me by the hand and led me to racks labeled
    "on sale"
Upon discovering they were made of a lesser quality, I started to wail

My pleas for prettier ones on display were ignored
Then she gave me one of her glaring looks while heading for the front door

Oh no! I couldn't leave empty-handed 'cause I really wanted new clothes
It took us years to get here, when another opportunity will come— who knows?

I yelled, "Look what I found, Mama! Isn't this nice?"
Holding up some ragamuffin dress with cats chasing mice

Grabbing stuff from the sales rack seemed to slow her pace
Despite being new, trying them on made me feel embarrassed and disgraced

Disappointed about arriving to school wearing stuff with no bling,
I pretended to like them when showing Mama how they looked
'Cause pleasing her was the most important thing

Just once I wanted to walk through school with swag, wearing the latest drip
Somehow while trying them on, I never noticed some had a few rips
Showing Mama the shabby quality and complaining my new clothes looked old
She suspected I tore them on purpose and, while paying, said gruffly, "Chil'
     let's go!"

Not Again, Georgy!

Georgy Porgy puddin' pie
Was rumored to have kissed the girls and made them cry

When the boys came out to play
Georgy Porgy always ran away

While strolling towards home
He felt sad and very alone

When, without warning,
Out of a big oak tree came bees a swarmin'

Georgy knew he had to think fast
Desperate to not get stung, he ran into oncoming traffic under an overpass

He ran all the way home, and was plumb out of breath
His mama glared at him and said, "I see you've gotten yourself into another
   mess!"

"Yesterday you were pestering the girls over near the Martin's place—
You're in trouble boy, I can see fear written on your face!"

Georgy Porgy tried, in vain, to explain
His mama said, "Whatever it is, I know you're to blame!"

"I got a call from Sara's mom and she sounded so miffed—
She claims you chased her girl. Did you ask her for a kiss?"

"I've warned you before, boy, you'd better cut that out!"
And in a thunderous voice she continued to shout

"Georgy Porgy puddin' pie,
If you even attempt to touch one more girl
You can pack your clothes... and go live with your Aunt Vie!"

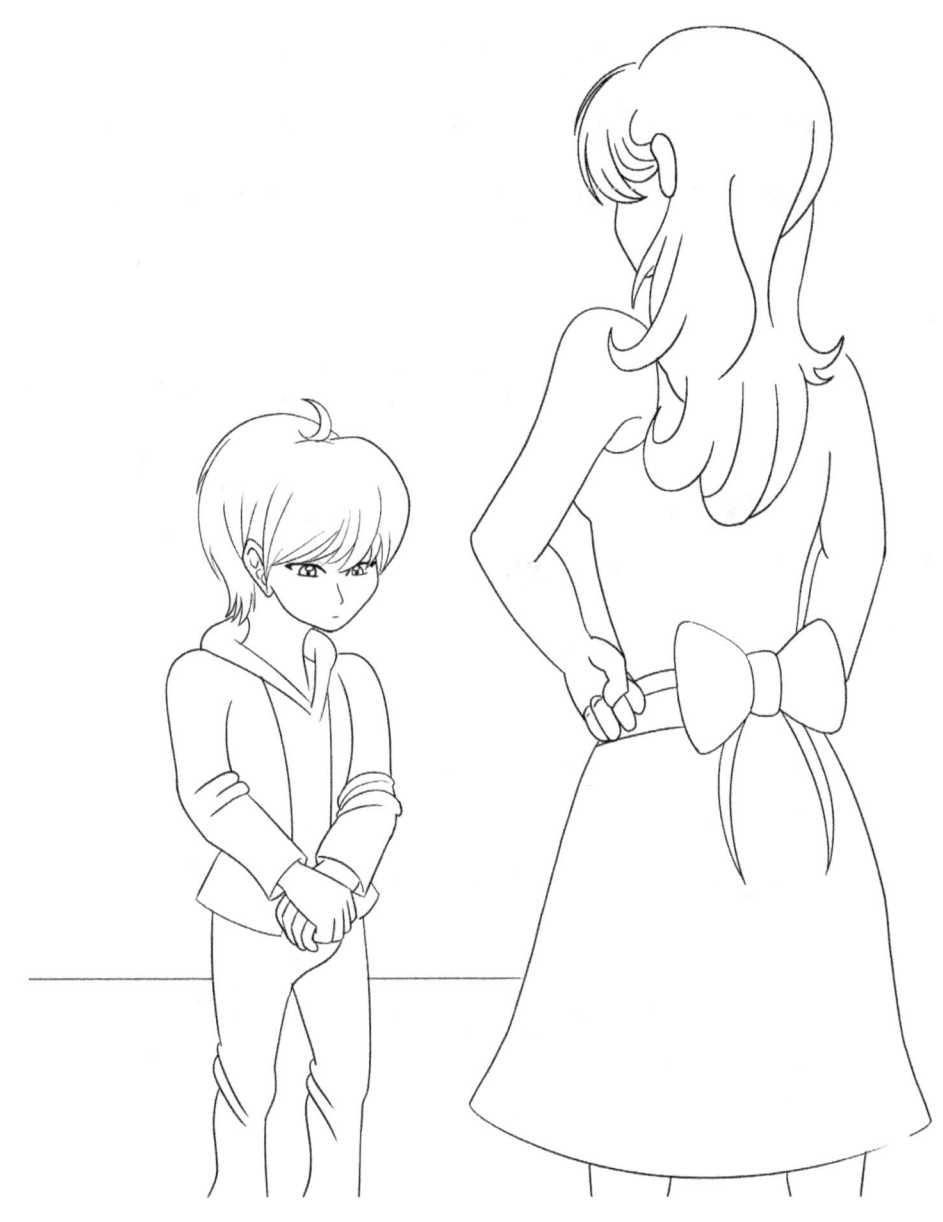

Math Can Be Perplexing

Multiplication is vexing

Division is as bad

The rule of three puzzles me

And practice drives me mad!

And while we're talking about learning

Let's just include those others subjects too

'Cause I swear I always feel so clueless

Every time my teacher introduces something new

Bedtime Is A Nightmare

The man in the moon looked out
    of the moon

Looked out of the moon and said,

"'Tis time for all children on Earth

To get immediately to bed!"

The man in the moon sounded like
    a bully

He spoke in a manner so mean

Which always makes kids defiant

'Cause when parents order them
    to bed, it's quite a scene

Honestly, who put him in charge
    of when kids should go to bed?

At the very least he could have spoken in a much gentler way

So when parents announce to kids that it's time for bed

Instead of fussing and cussing, they'll hear,

"Okay, and thanks for a wonderful day!"

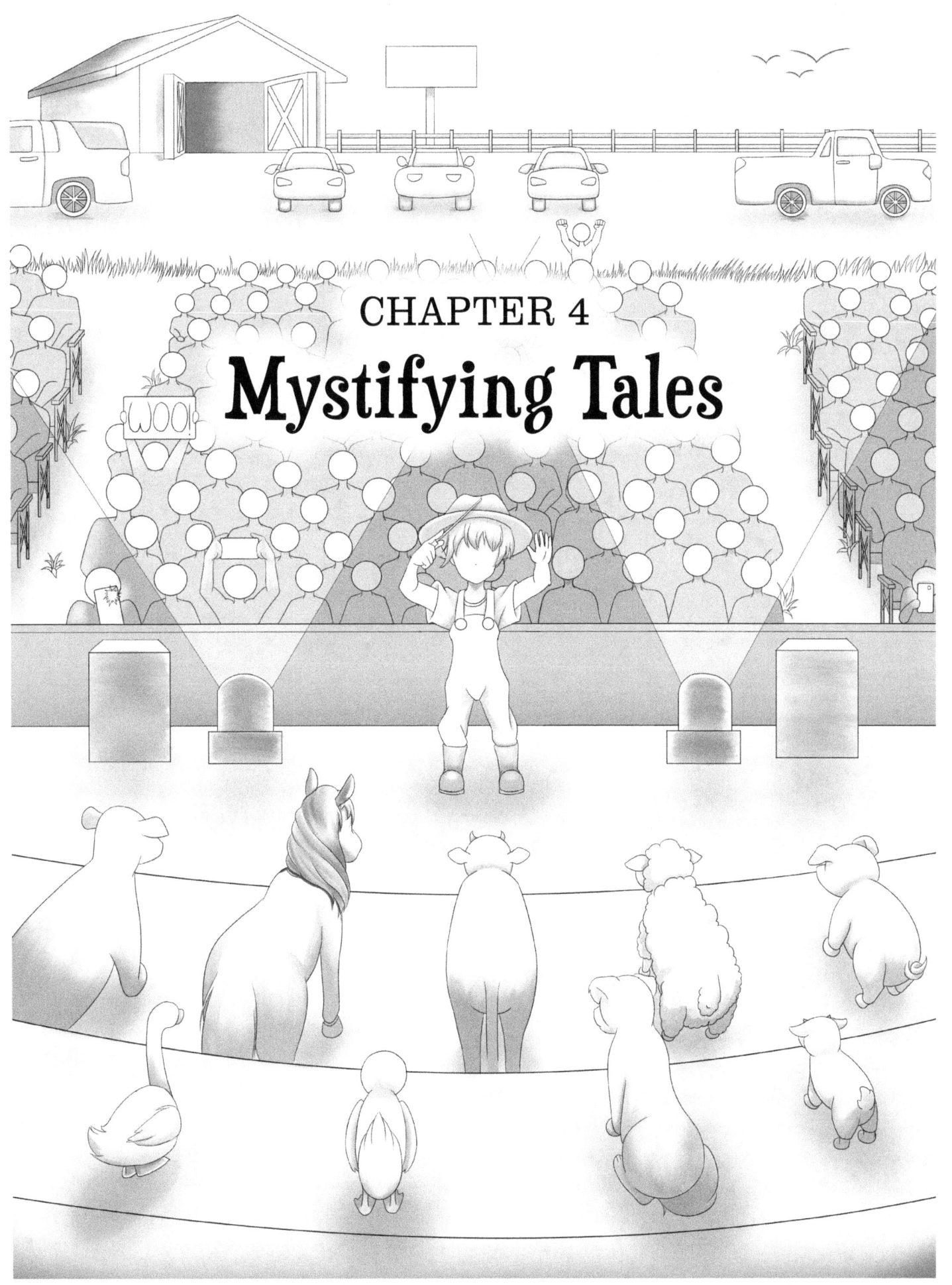

CHAPTER 4
Mystifying Tales

Some Things Make No Sense

See, see! What shall I see?

A horse's head where his tail should be.

Hey, that sounds backwards, I don't understand...

Anything is possible with a pen in one's hand!

Old Innovative MacDonald
(Put some respect on his name!)

Old MacDonald has a farm
E-I-E-I-O
I was given directions to this mysterious place
But I'm not really sure I'm gonna go

Even though I am rather curious
His farm is kind of far
And good directions don't matter
If you don't have a dependable car

Gosh, I'm so torn about this trip
'Cause his place has such a reputation
Traffic gets backed up for miles
Visitors eager to see cows rumored to be a singing sensation

Imagine animals putting on a musical show!
With altos and sopranos all singing in key
Belting out songs Mac taught them
In perfect harmony

Did you know their tunes are so popular
They were invited to the Grammys to sing their biggest hit?
Apparently they tend to poop while singing
Which panicked front row dignitaries, scattering to find somewhere else to sit

Old MacDonald's farm may smell a bit funky
Most visitors plug their noses while passing through,
But as unpleasant as folks may find the odor,
I hear sessions are sold out every afternoon by two

Miss Muffet's Chill Time Interrupted

Little Miss Muffet
Sat on a tuffet
Eating some curds and whey
There came a female spider
Who quietly sat down beside her
But frightened Miss Muffet away

She shouted, "No wait! Please don't run away
I just wandered down to ask you to play!"

Oh, how she hated a spider's reputation!
Feeling frustrated, she sat and began a long
    period of contemplation
And with a burst of sudden inspiration
She happened upon an idea she thought
    worthy of serious consideration

"Perhaps if I disguise myself as something other than a spider. But what
    shall I be?
Hmm... let me think a minute... now, let's see...

I could become a cat because people enjoy hearing them purr
How I envy the warm, playful way people gently rub a cat's fur!
Or a puppy, they're so doggone cute and popular
Some pets live in cages, which makes me wonder if they feel more secure?

We spiders are fairly low maintenance; just need some space to build a web
Finding and gathering our own source of food is done by planning ahead

Occasionally we're known to travel up and down waterspouts
If our appearance is unexpected, we make some people wanna shout
(It's kind of entertaining watching them panic and flail all about)
When I'm spotted casually strutting up walls or across floors people just
     flip out...

Running from basements, attics, kitchens, and even bathtubs...
     often forgetting their towels.
The reactions we get are so funny; it makes us laugh and howl!

What will it take to convince you that spiders make good non-traditional pets?
We quietly travel through spaces so cool and calm. We're really no threat
And think of the cost saving fees, since we don't require visits to the vet!
So few people seem to appreciate how we keep them safe from other pests

It makes a spider wonder, from our dark corners and tight spaces,
Would people miss us if we packed up our webs and moved to more welcoming
     places?

Jack's New Jingle

Little Jack Jingle
Used to live single
Until he met his true soul mate
Both now live together
And are reaping the mutual
    rewards forever
Because being two halves of a
    whole feels so great

When one is fortunate to find a loving companion
Although unspoken, they'll never fear being abandoned
It's the special relationship so many patiently await
Poor Jack, who often lamented he might never find
That special someone to whom his heart might bind
Was unexpectedly rewarded with a joyous fate

He must remember to send a message of thanks
To the pet shelter uniting him with Bo-janks
So grateful is he for their compatibility
Greeted at home with unconditional love,
A wagging tail and eager nose nudging for pats and warm hugs
He can hardly wait for the end of each workday at three!

Why We Should Listen to Wise Old Owls

A wise old owl sat in an oak
The more he heard, the less
    he spoke;
The less he spoke, the more
    he heard
Why aren't we all like that
    wise old bird?

I suspect the answer lies in our need to pontificate
Who among us can resist a hearty debate?
We might all benefit from resisting the impulse for the last word
Because it wouldn't hurt to *shush* and listen before blurting something absurd

For some, it is about one-upmanship
Winning at all costs, ignoring cues to quit
Bantering or jousting may gratify some souls
Overlooking the need for humility when coming out on top is one's ultimate goal

Quietly listening without need to retort
Allows us to hear others in need of support
For wisdom to contend with life's ups and downs
We should learn to read the needs of one wearing a frown

It takes strength to admit you don't know it all
So the next time someone cares enough to give you a call
Ask them how they are, and just listen to what they need from you
To help them navigate when they're feeling unsure about what to do.

CHAPTER 5
Expect The Unexpected

What's Taffy Up To Now?

Taffy is my neighbor
He's also a thief
Taffy came to my house
And stole a piece of beef

But Taffy must have felt something
About stealing from the poor
Because he had a change of heart
And returned it to my back door

In fact, he also left some potatoes
String beans and sweet cornbread
Which I truly appreciated
'Cause I never felt so well-fed

So Taffy's changed his ways
No longer 'round here and up to no good—
But rumor has it he still steals from others
Who live in more wealthy neighborhoods

When Punch Punched Judy

Punch and Judy
Fought for a pie
Punch gave Judy
A knock to the eye

"Geez!" said Judy,
"You never fight fair!"
Punch shrugged his shoulders
And, with indifference, said, "I don't care."

Judy started fuming
Boy she really felt dissed
She took a swing at Punch
But her right upper-cut missed

Punch jumped out of the way
Dodging to his left, then right
Judy, determined as ever,
Charged at him with all of her might

Punch made a mistake
Deciding to take Judy's anger lightly
While grabbing his head, she asked, "Who's in charge now?"
Then body slammed him without apology

Grunting and groaning loudly
They tossed one another around
By the end of their sibling struggle
Punch laid with his face to the ground

Judy held him there tightly
Her grip on him a bit rough
When Punch started sobbing
She asked, "Have you had enough?"

"Yes, yes I give up!"
Punch acquiesced with a sob
Humiliation was added to his physical pain
When he noticed the onlooking mob

Simon's Accidental Encounter

Simple Simon met a pieman
Going to the fair
Says Simple Simon to the pieman,
How much would it cost for me to buy this pie here?

He only meant to point at it,
But Simon accidentally pushed his finger in
Realizing what he had done
He said "Oops" and apologized with a sheepish grin

The pieman wasn't amused
No, not the least little bit
Turning red in the face, he angrily yelled
"You'll have to pay for that!", while spraying spit

Simple Simon said to the pieman
"Really, mister, it was an accident!
And besides, it isn't all that noticeable—
I barely made a small dent!"

"You don't understand the point,"
Said the pieman, "My reputation's at stake.
I'm known all across the countryside
For the perfection of every pie I bake."

The pieman informed Simple Simon
The cost of the pie was five dollars and fifty cents
Simple Simon turned his pockets inside and out
The pieman stared, exasperated, 'cause he knew what the inside-out meant

Anticipating a loss of profit
Knowing that pie wouldn't be fit for his display case
The pieman brainstormed for some ideas
On how to recoup from a potential waste

He proposed some form of bartering
Explaining to Simple Simon the payback
He would take this menace and convert him into his apprentice
Simon responded with, "Yeah, I could do that."

After days of working together
Simon showed promise in the work that he did
One day when they were closing up shop
The pieman casually asked, "How'd you like to make this permanent, kid?"

Simple Simon couldn't believe his luck for a chance to earn a buck
Without hesitation he said, "Yes!" and they shook with a firm grip
The pieman had an ulterior motive, though:
He'd grown fond of Simon's companionship

Three Cats of Kilkenny Are One Too Many

There were once three cats of Kilkenny
Each thought there was one cat too many
So they constantly hissed and spit
When close, they scratched and they bit.

Hissing and howling till they grew too weary to fight
They finally decided to call a truce for the night
Crawling to spaces of comfort, each to his or her own favorite spot
Thinking a good night's rest would rejuvenate their strength—
But. It. Did. Not.

At first sign of daylight each woke to stretch, but could only moan
One of them screamed, "Yikes! I think I've broken a bone!"
All moved about using careful steps, feeling trepidation
Not in a hurry to resume last night's scurry, they yowled to project intimidation.

Circling one another and whipping their tails,
Periodically stopping to sharpen and prune their nails,
Arching their backs and opening their mouths wide,
The cats appeared anything but wimpy, 'cause they had cat pride!

Each took the fight stance, hunching down low and preparing to leap
But deep in their hearts, they secretly longed to be meek
But no such luck— despite their waiting, it was a temporary stand-off
Any moment the tussle would begin again with cat fur flying aloft.

Oh yeah, they were ready, each prepared to gouge out eyes
Conjuring images of victory, meowing the other's demise;
Should they approach from the rear to avoid a claw to the face,
Or just mount the other nitwit and grip firmly to their waist?

Glaring, one cat at the other, wondering who would be the one to start?
When one of them emitted something that sounded like a fart
All three scattered 'cause none were willing to take
the blame
Then an argument ensued with each
calling the other names.

One angrily asked, "Which of
you two funky monkeys let
one loose?"
"Excuse me Mr. Repugnant?" replied
the gray striped cat while sipping spilled juice.
"I delay using the kitty litter after you're done 'cause the stank is so bad!"
The third cat refused to admit he was the culprit 'cause he liked making the
others mad.

And on and on they argued; their response always disproportionate to the event
Nonetheless, the spat proceeded until the two were completely spent
Could it be a momentary truce disguised as a catnap?
Even with eyelids closed their rapid eye movement hinted of dreams of the
next attack.

Curiously though, the grogginess of sleep served a purpose of another kind
While purring softly, they began to rethink the notion of kicking another's
behind
As nature would have it, they yearned for comfort, and snuggled closer to
each other,
Like magnets they clung and cuddled as children would with their mother.

Ahh yes, this was truly what they had preferred all along:
The opportunity for peace and to purr a harmonious song.
Occasionally, one would awake and cuddle closer, their bodies intertwined
Huddled in quiet repose, with no sign that a few minutes ago, fighting was on
their mind.

To Market With A List,
But Where's My Map?

To market, to market to buy a fat pig
Home again, home again jiggety jig

Wait a minute, whoa! I think I lost my map...
I'm fairly new to these parts, I need my directions to help me keep track

Now let me see, where did I put the dumb thing?
Maybe by the cashier's counter near the register— I remember hearing it ring

Sure, sure it must have fallen on the floor,
Or I might have even dropped it near the door

Of course, I could have left it in the produce between the mushrooms and
    avocados —
And such an inconvenient time to lose it! I have to pee; I mean, I really gotta go!

Standing here with my legs tightly crossed feeling very perplexed
And not a soul in sight to point me towards home— gosh what'll I do next?

Well, I paid dearly for my indecisiveness, my reaction time too late,
As a warm liquid trickled down and I walked home with a strange gait

And wouldn't you know it, when I needed someone no one was around
But after the map mishap, I encountered almost every person in town

I just kept walking funny, catching the tail-end of their talking and many
    giggles;
I even met my teacher, Ms. Farthington, who commented on my wiggle

I tried to play the whole thing off, you know, pretend they hadn't really
   noticed me,
But with a herd of flies gathered around my legs, that was a short-lived fantasy

So now, I'm hobblin' and stankin' like pee, swatting flies left and right
All the time smiling, greeting folks with false pleasantries, my pants getting
   too tight

Upon finding my way, my pants started to dry, so now I'm wishing myself thin,
'Cause I'm starting to feel a rash and painful chaffing of my skin

Keeping my composure is the toughest thing to do
As I'm reduced to waving with one hand while mumbling,
                    "Hi! And how are you?"

                    The other hand is down my pants to alleviate the itch;
                       Beyond embarrassed, I desperately want to hide, but
                          without my map, I can't even find the nearest ditch!

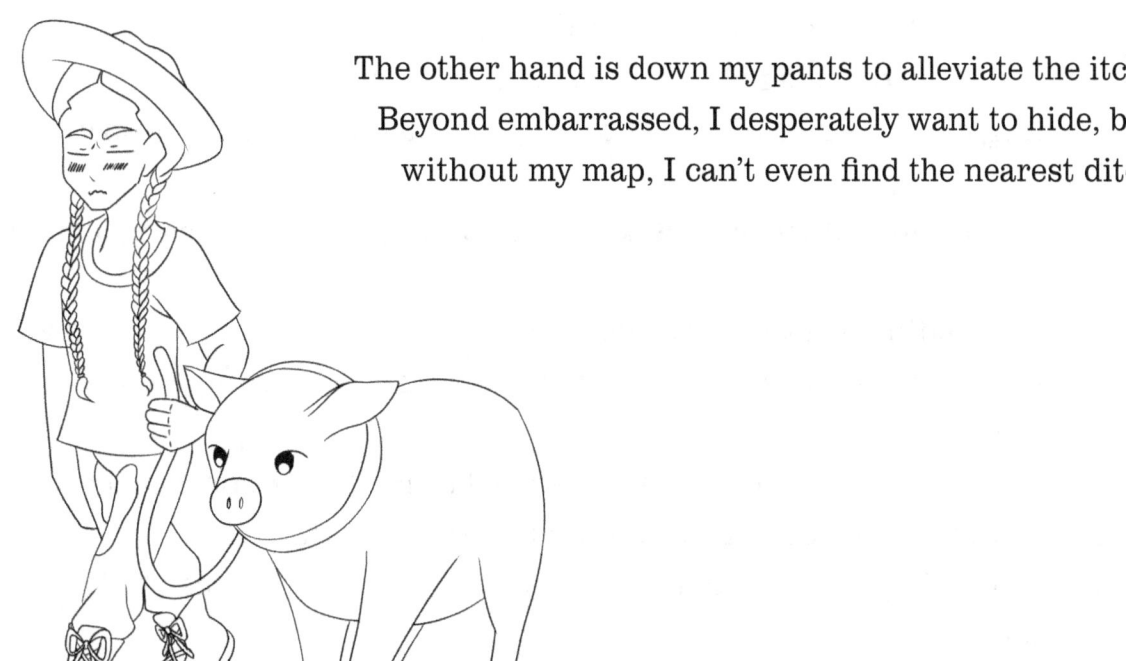

Little Tee Wee's BIG Adventure At Sea

Little Tee Wee
She went to the sea
In an open boat,
And while afloat,
Spotted a menacing shark

She pulled in her net,
Which was heavy and wet,
And the shark's fin
    became entangled;
Not wanting it to panic
    and become mangled
Tee Wee had to think fast
    to free it before dark

Harkening back to times of fishing with her dad
She recalled a similar experience they both once had
When he mysteriously managed to first cajole then calm the beast
Disentangling it had seemed effortless to him, but that didn't help her now in
    the least;
Compassion made her all the more determined to free it without leaving a mark

The sun began setting, emitting various hues of red
Wondering about the initial steps her father took, she tried sorting it out
    in her head.
Finally recalling his actions in sequence, remembering distraction was the key,
She immediately started tossing the day's catch back into the sea
Despite the prickling sensation of fraying nerves, her faculties remained
    razor sharp

The boat quietly drifted, and she felt an eerie sensation— how calm the shark
      remained!
This was gonna go better than she had anticipated, but could she rely on
      it staying tame?
Proceeding with the task of tossing while disentangling the net in a
      casual stride
The only unexpected glitch was the presence of another shark off the
      starboard side.
Struck with panic she wondered, "What'll I do now?" wishing she could hide
      under a tarp

She managed to free the first shark, which brought relief— wow,
      it's finally over!
But the two sharks huddled closer to the boat; her moment of joy
      turned sober
Frozen to her seat, instinctively she knew to stay still and oh so quiet
Hoping not to spark their hunger so she could avoid being part of today's diet
Tee Wee knew if she made any sudden moves, they would attack her on a lark

She couldn't just do nothing! Frustration mounted while sharks floated
      beside her;
Intending to high-tail it out of there required some form of distraction—
      a pacifier.
Unable to think clearly, she suddenly grasped the oars and held on tight
Lowering them to the water, she pushed panic aside and thought singing
      might reduce her fright
Overcome by confusion, she thought of a song, but almost forgot where
      to start

"I will row, row, row this boat, but prefer it was powered with steam,

Wearily, wearily, wearily, wearily, I wish this were a dream!"

Glancing from bow to stern, hoping she hadn't attracted their attention,

She maintained a calm pace, grimacing all the while through so much fear
and tension.

Determined to safely arrive at her destination, attending to the course she
did chart

Gradually, she put a considerable amount of distance between her and
her foes;

Tempted to loosen her grip just a bit, but her mind begged her hands to
not let go.

Eventually, she eased up, but maintained her rhythm, she settled into
her groove—

Alas, she finally spotted land and held fast to the oars; undaunted,
she continued to move

Feeling elated in anticipation of achieving the mission on which she did
embark

Just when she thought she had nothing left 'cause her muscles were
racked with pain,

The boat struck a sand bar, which unleashed a gush of tears she mistook
for rain.

The combination of relief and grief overwhelmed her with profound
appreciation

For what her beloved father had passed on: an appreciation of their
habitation.

Little Tee Wee lived to sail again 'cause her father had also taught her
to be smart

Acknowledgments

As always I first acknowledge those credited on the opening page of my books for their contributions. However, given the enormity of the *Wait...Who Got Goosed?*™ project, the usual message of "thanks" feels insufficient. The successful publication of my first poetry book and companion activity book was truly a unique experience. One of the most rewarding parts of the journey was the opportunity to work with a collaborative of gifted artists, editors, book and graphic designers. Their contributions were so invaluable I feel are they are deserving of greater appreciation.

Writing a contemporary version of Mother Goose Rhymes was an aspiration kept quietly under wraps, until now. Launching Pivot In New Directions Publishing provided an opportunity to reintroduce myself as a writer of stories through rhymes. But the successful production of *Wait...Who Got Goosed?*™ poetry book and Companion Activity Book required the assistance of uniquely qualified individuals.

Graphic artist Kitten Saphire contributed amazing illustrations for book covers, as well as scenes, capturing the characters and events in a way that demonstrated her ability to grasp and visually represent the essence of each poem. Kitten Saphire also illustrated the companion activity book.

The first step in this process, however, was having poems originally written on a typewriter (I'll describe what a typewriter is at another time) transcribed into a Word document. After numerous rounds of updating and *DIY* editing, it was time to enlist the support of professional editors and proofreaders.

As a writer of three education books, my transition from writing about education to writing a contemporary version of Mother Goose Rhymes required the services of an editor and proofreader familiar with the nuances of poetry.

Venturing into writing poetry was so much fun— at first! Initially, I was unencumbered by the presence of editors, proof-readers, and their rules. Upon receiving my first draft of edited poems, a new round of work began; the editor's comments hinted that I possessed the makings of a poet, but I still had quite a ways to grow. Having access to resourceful friends like *Merriam and Webster* (any time I encountered unfamiliar concepts) was very helpful in deciphering the meaning of each area of development. I eventually learned to value the editors' critiques as constructive recommendations, intended to transform me from a thin-skinned sensitive writer into a better storyteller. I am so grateful for their guidance and how they challenged me to think a little deeper. Their editorial probes elevated the quality of my narrative skills.

Proudly, I want to share that almost the entire network of collaborators, for the *Wait...Who Got Goosed?*™ project included educators. Editor Lisa Shrewsberry is a school teacher and part-time professor. Proofreader Madison McMillion has taught the art of writing poetry to children in Montana and is, at present, work-ing with the Teach For America Program. Former schoolteachers Talya Marshall and Whitney Marshall remain active in teaching. Book designer Michelle M. White's education background includes writing and homeschooling as well as publishing the Keynote Classics™ series of books (annotated classic literature with an added Introductory Key, explanatory footnotes, and discussion/ study questions designed to help students and casual readers gain a deeper understanding of often complex period literature).

Readers will appreciate why I felt so fortunate to have the extraordinary support of educators gifted in other skills to work with me on the *Wait...Who Got Goosed?*™ project. What began as a mission of one evolved into a collective mission. It was an abso-lute pleasure and honor working with members of this team. Many thanks to each of you!

About the Author

Over the past few years, author Julie Coles has enjoyed opportunities to dip her toes into new literary waters. Growing beyond her role as a self-published writer to owning two publishing companies, Julie presents her most recent company, Pivot In New Directions, as a symbol of her decision to shift and allow herself to wonder *What If?* about her other areas of interest. Being a habitual daydreamer of innovative ideas has served Julie well as a former teacher, consultant, and school leader. The same *What If?* machine keeps on running, providing the impetus for her most recent writing pursuits. While reading for what felt like for the umpteenth time *Mother Goose Nursery Rhymes*, Julie experienced one of those *What If?* moments.

Inspired by the centuries-old fables about past human foibles, Julie reimagined a contemporary version of those popular fables. Introducing new characters who, like their predecessors in the original Mother Goose Rhymes, possess questionable decision-making skills, Julie thought people today might enjoy poetic narratives shared in the context of our contemporary language and situations.

While writing her new version of poems, Julie found the experience to be hilarious, which greatly influenced her lyrical levity. Discovering that what oftentimes makes lessons more memorable is in how stories are shared, Julie felt no hesitation about infusing generous amounts of humor. If readers experience joy while reading Julie's contemporary tales, she will have achieved what she set out to do: captivate others' imagination through storytelling and a healthy dose of humor. Readers are meant to enjoy this book!

Be sure to purchase *Wait...Who Got Goosed?*™ Companion Activity Book.

Activities include projects tailored to Budding Young Poets, Math Wizards, and Artists. Each of the activity zones features engaging and fun ways to use your imagination. You don't need to be a poet, math wizard or artist to enjoy activities designed for anyone who is curious.

Imagine becoming the main character in Little Laid Back Bo-Peep and other poems in the Budding Young Poets activity zone, where you are the star. Then you get to fill in missing words that rhyme with other words in many poems.

Your wisdom will be needed for the Budding Young Math Wizards zone. Math Wizards are like detectives who solve mysterious problems. For example, if 10 sheep worth $50.00 wander off, my goodness....what is the total cost of the income lost by villagers who own those sheep? And...if each of the 10 sheep purchases a passport for $25.00 and escapes to another country, what is the total cost for the passports purchased by the 10 sheep? That's two important mysteries villagers need your help solving. You'll need to put on your thinking cap to solve those and other mysterious math problems linked with *Wait...Who Got Goosed?* poems.

Your time in the Budding Young Artist Zone will be another adventure. There are no rules. You get to choose your art tools of choice and unleash your creative side. Drawing outside the lines is welcome and encouraged.

The Wait...Who Got Goosed Companion Activity Book will be a delightful experience especially for 3rd graders through middle grade students. But it's also for the kid inside of everyone, regardless of our age.